CONTENTS

Published 2024. Little Brother Books Ltd, Ground Floor, 23 Southernhay East, Exeter, Devon EX1 1QL
books@littlebrotherbooks.co.uk | www.littlebrotherbooks.co.uk
Printed in the United Kingdom
The Little Brother Books trademark, email and website addresses, are the sole and exclusive properties of Little Brother Books Limited.

ONLINE ACTIVITIES

On some of the pages you will see QR codes. These QR codes take you to online Purple Mash activities which support learning from the relevant page.

To use the QR codes, scan the QR code with the camera on your web enabled tablet, click on the link and the activity will appear on screen.

Alternatively, QR readers are available on the app store for your device.

SCAN CODE

purple mash

PARTS OF A SENTENCE!

The Angry Birds are an elite squad of feathered friends. They each have their own name and a special skill too.

> **Nouns** are words that refer to a person, place, thing or event. **Verbs** are action or doing words.

1

Look at the words below. Can you identify the **nouns** and **verbs**? Circle all the **nouns** and underline all the **verbs**.

egg	Chuck	flying	breaking	smashing

pig	beak	feathers	catapult	building	snout

sunglasses   eyebrows   tower   angrily   bricks

Red   door   snorting   trotters   Bomb   exploding

moustache   catching   playing   Matilda   squawking

2

Adjectives are used to describe the noun in more detail.

*The pigs have built an **enormous** tower.*

Underline the **adjective** in these sentences:

a. Red's black eyebrows help him show how angry he is.

b. Bomb makes a huge explosion.

c. The catapult is super stretchy.

d. The birds think their eggs are very precious.

e. Matilda is the calmest bird on the block... until she's not.

> **Tower** is the noun so **enormous** is the adjective because it describes the tower.

3

Adverbs describe the word in the sentence that is the verb, an adjective or another adverb. They give information about the action such as how, when or where the action was done.

*Chuck moves **fast** through the air.*

Fast is the **adverb**; it explains how Chuck moves.

Use an **adverb** to complete these sentences:

a. The pigs build their towers _____ .

b. The Blues land _____ .

c. Red leads the birds _____ .

d. Silver _____ works on her homework.

ANGRY BIRDS

HANDWRITING PRACTICE

The pigs have to design new towers so quickly that sometimes their plans are hard to read!

Ascenders include all capital letters and the lower-case letters which reach the top line such as l, t and k. Descenders sit on the line, but part fall below the line you are writing on, such as p, q and g. When handwriting, you must ensure that you space your words out so that the ascenders of the line below do not obstruct the descenders from the line above.

1 Practise writing out the **ascenders** and **descenders**. Be sure they are spaced appropriately.

Ascenders

b   d   h   k   l   t

Descenders

g   p   q   y

2 Leonard is trying to work out the words the pigs have written on the blueprints. Can you help him by writing out the words in your best handwriting?

Wooden   hammer   nails

3

HOMOPHONES AND NEAR HOMOPHONES

The Hatchlings may look similar, but trust us - they are adorable in their own unique way! A near homophone is a word which is pronounced almost the same as another word, but it has a different spelling and meaning.

> **Homophones** are words that sound the same but have different spellings and meanings. A **near homophone** is a word which is pronounced almost the same as another word but has a different spelling and meaning.

1 Help the Hatchlings to make a match. Draw a line to link the **homophones**. The first one has been done for you.

pear   meat   ball   break   great   herd   knight   blue

bawl   night   pair   brake   heard   blew   meet   grate

2 Circle the **homophone** which makes these sentences correct.

a. Terence wants to **meet / meat** Matilda by the pond.

b. The pigs **herd / heard** Chef Pig had a new recipe for cooking grass!

c. Silver's experiment **blue / blew** up.

d. King Pig has a **grate / great** plan for his next attack!

e. Hal **mist / missed** the pigs tower.

3 Write out the pairs of **near homophones** next to each other in the table. The first one has been done for you.

Near homophones

quiet	quite

quiet   were   further   accept   bury

berry   father   where   except   quite

READING COMPREHENSION

Matilda has been feeling anxious. Read the text below then answer the questions about it. Remember to pay attention to the details of what you read and develop a picture of it in your head – this will help you to understand the text better.

MATILDA'S PRESENT

Matilda had been feeling very worried and anxious. Terence wanted to buy a present for Matilda to show her how much he cared for her. But, it's not easy for a big guy who doesn't like to show his emotions or, you know, speak at all! He decided to ask Chuck to help him choose the perfect present. First they went to the bakery. Terence pointed to a huge cream cake, but Chuck reminded Terence that Matilda prefers to bake her own cakes. Next, they went to the Bird Boutique. Terence pointed out a lovely new set of pearls, but Chuck thought they were too expensive. Finally, they went to the Bubble Tea stand. Terence was sure Matilda would love a Berry Blast, but Chuck thought Matilda was allergic to berries.

Feeling frustrated, Terence went home, alone. Sitting in his house, Terence thought of the perfect present for Matilda. He went to her house the next day and simply sat quietly while Matilda flapped around him, telling him all her latest news and worries. After an hour, Matilda truly was a Zen Hen.

1 Answer the true or false questions by putting a tick in the correct box.

	TRUE	FALSE
a. Terence wanted to buy Chuck a present.		
b. They went to the bakery first.		
c. Terence wanted to buy a loaf of bread.		
d. Matilda likes to bake her own cakes.		
e. Chuck thought pearls were too expensive.		
f. Chuck thought Matilda was allergic to berries.		

2 Write a sentence to answer these questions.

a. Which three shops did Terence and Chuck visit?

_____

b. Why did Terence want to help Matilda?

_____

c. What did Terence give Matilda in the end?

_____

DIRECT SPEECH

There is always plenty of direct speech when the pigs are building towers!

Leonard gathered the Bad Piggies together. It was early in the morning and they had a huge tower to build.

"I want this tower built by lunchtime!" said Leonard.

"Will we get extra portions if we do?" said a Bad Piggy.

This is an example of direct speech. Direct speech is a way to write exactly what the characters in the story say.

Here are some tips for writing direct speech:

Speech marks: The words that are spoken are punctuated with inverted commas.

New speaker, new line: Each time the speaker changes, you should start a new line to make it clear that a different person is speaking.

Reporting clause: This is the writing that says who has spoken, there should be punctuation (a comma, question mark, exclamation mark etc.) between the direct speech and the reporting clause.

1 Punctuate these direct speech sentences by putting in their missing inverted commas around the spoken words. The first one has been done for you.

a. "I need a new job, fast!" said Chef Pig.

b. Is anyone paying attention to my latest invention? asked Garry.

c. Has anyone seen my phone charger? asked Courtney.

d. Nearly time for lunch! said Chef Pig.

e. I need more eggs! shouted Leonard.

2 You can make your direct speech more interesting for the reader by not always using the word 'said' in the reporting clause.

How many other words could you use?

whispered
cried
shouted

TNT

INDEFINATE ARTICLES

ANGRY BIRDS

Pig City is THE place to hang out if you are a pig with personality.

Articles refer to items (nouns) when talking or writing. There are **definite articles**, such as **the** table (meaning a specific table) and **indefinite articles** of **a** or **an**, such as **a** pen (meaning any pen). If a word starts with a **vowel sound**, use **an** and if the word starts with a **consonant** sound, use **a**.

1 Courtney has taken a picture to upload to her social media page.
Choose **6 items**, add them to the list and use the correct **indefinite article** for each item.

_____ _____

_____ _____

_____ _____

2 Some words start with a letter which makes a sound different to its letter sound.

For example: 'It was an **honest mistake**.' The h makes a vowel sound 'o' so you use 'an' despite 'h' being a consonant. Put 'a' or 'an' before these words.

Top tip: listen carefully to the starting sound of the word before you decide.

a. **x-ray**   b. **honour**   c. **uniform**   d. **hour**

SPELLING PATTERN -CIAN

The Hatchlings are deciding which jobs they would like to be when they grow up - apart from pig-busting, flying machines of course...

Most words have spelling patterns. Words with the -cian spelling pattern often indicate a skilled occupation.

1 Add the **-cian** ending to these occupations.
Draw a line to match the occupation with the description.

a. An eye specialist   physi _____

b. A doctor   beauti _____

c. Plays an instrument   magi _____

d. Performs tricks   electri _____

e. Works with electricity   opti _____

f. Works with makeup   musi _____

2 Unscramble these occupations using the hints:

a. Elected to run the country   **ploitician** _____

b. Very good with numbers   **iahetmmtacian** _____

c. Might fix the computers at school **iecthncian** _____

d. Advises on healthy eating   **eidtician** _____

8

SIMILIES

The birds glide like soaring angels, the pigs fall like heavy stones! Meanwhile, the eggs just sit there, waiting to be rescued, like trapped princesses.

When writing descriptively, you can use similes to help the reader develop a picture of what is happening. Similes compare something with something else and use the word as or like.

1 Match the **simile** to the correct bird. The first one has been done for you.

As red as a ripe cherry.

Loves her eggs as much as mice love cheese.

A beak as big as a boomerang

Louder than thunder.

Proud as a peacock.

As fast as lightning.

Red   **Bomb**   **Matilda**   **Hal**   **Mighty Eagle**   **Chuck**

2 Practise writing a few **similes** here. The first one has been done for you.

a. Leonard is as happy as a ___**kid at Christmas**___ when he has eggs to hoard.

b. Leonard is as angry as a _____ when the Bad Piggies don't behave.

c. Courtney loves her phone like a _____ .

d. Garry is as clever as a _____ when he comes up with a new idea.

e. Chef Pig is as cross as a _____ when no one pays attention to him.

ALPHABETICAL ORDER

Red has decided the birds need to be more organised. He's going to put all the birds in alphabetical order.

Alphabetical order is an ordering system whereby words are put into an order based on their first letter and that letter's position in the alphabet.

To order bananas, apples and cherries, we would look at each word's initial letter. Apples would be first as 'a' is the first letter in the alphabet, bananas would be second and cherries third.

1

Matilda　　　**Hal**　　　**Stella**

Put the birds into alphabetical order:

1. _____
2. _____
3. _____

2

When there are words which start with the same letter, look at the second letter of the words to order them. Silver would come before Stella in alphabetical order as the **second** letter of Silver's name is 'i' which comes before 't' in the alphabet.

Put the birds into alphabetical order:

Bomb　　　**Bubbles**　　　**Blues**

1. _____　　2. _____

3. _____

3

When the first and second letters are the same, look at the **third** letter to indicate the alphabetical order.

Put these birds into alphabetical order:

Chloe　　　**Chuck**

1. _____
2. _____

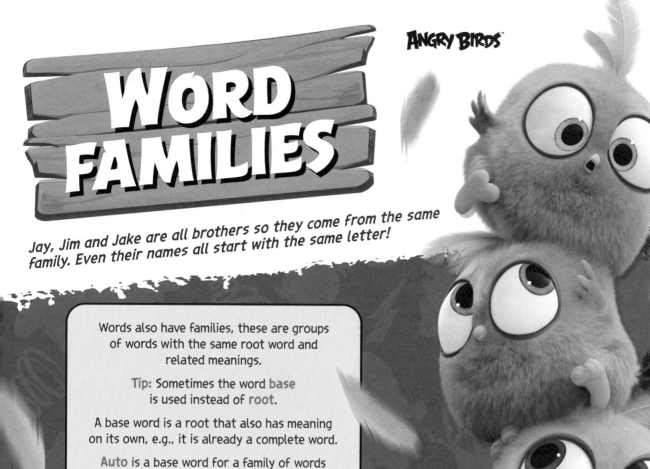

WORD FAMILIES

ANGRY BIRDS

Jay, Jim and Jake are all brothers so they come from the same family. Even their names all start with the same letter!

Words also have families, these are groups of words with the same root word and related meanings.

Tip: Sometimes the word base is used instead of root.

A base word is a root that also has meaning on its own, e.g., it is already a complete word.

Auto is a base word for a family of words such as automatic, automobile, automated. They have similar meanings.

1 Sort the words below into their families.

tricycle   television   triangle   microscope   telescope
telephone   microphone   tripod   microwave

Family 1   **Family 2**   **Family 3**

_____   _____   _____
_____   _____   _____
_____   _____   _____

2 The Blues have worked out the meaning of the base word for each family. Can you draw lines to match the base words to their family meaning?

micro   distant

tri   small

tele   three

PREFIXES

SCAN CODE

purple mash

The most important thing for the birds is to make the pigs' tower unstable and get their eggs back!

A **prefix** is a group of letters put in front of a root (or base) word. The prefix 'un' turns a stable tower into something far more wobbly!

1

Circle the **prefix** on all of these words. The first one has been done for you.

(super)market   midnight   impossible   impolite

indoors   misplace   superstar   incomplete

superman   unusual   nonsense   unequal

2

Complete the chart:

Prefix	Root word	New word
super	man	superman
_____	write	rewrite
in	dependent	_____
im	mature	_____
_____	patient	impatient
super	_____	superstar
non	sense	_____
_____	equal	unequal

DIRECT SPEECH

Hal is entertaining the birds with some funny jokes. He uses direct speech to help him remember each one.

When speech is written down, it is called direct speech. Here is a reminder of our direct speech top tips:

Speech marks: The words that are spoken are punctuated with inverted commas.

New speaker, new line: Each time the speaker changes, you should start a new line to make it clear that a different person is speaking.

Reporting clause: This is the writing that says who has spoken, there should be punctuation (a comma, question mark, exclamation mark etc.) between the direct speech and the reporting clause.

Inverted commas go directly around the actual words being said by the character. Punctuation, such as a question mark, is placed inside the inverted commas. Imagine a speech bubble – the inverted commas act like a speech bubble.

1 These are Hal's two favourite jokes. Can you write the joke conversations below using inverted commas and the correct punctuation.

a. Hal asked, what did Matilda say to the cat about their handwriting? I don't know sighed Red it's paw-fect! snorted Hal

b. What is sticky and brown? Hal giggled I don't know, you tell me! Red replied A stick! Hahaha! laughed Hal

2 Rewrite Riley and Will's conversation into direct speech with inverted commas.
Top tip: Be sure to use interesting words instead of said!

I've got a great idea, let's sneak up to eagle mountain!

Excellent idea! We can listen to all of Mighty Eagle's interesting stories.

READING COMPREHENSION

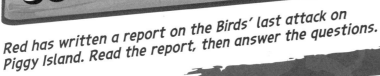

Red has written a report on the Birds' last attack on Piggy Island. Read the report, then answer the questions.

RED'S REPORT

In our latest attack on Piggy Island, we wanted to get five eggs back from the stinking green pigs. We can't let them take our precious eggs and cuter than cute hatchlings!

Chuck went first, but he flew so fast he missed the island completely. We are still waiting for him to get back. Next up was supposed to be Mighty Eagle, but he was too busy telling the Blues a story and missed the flight time.

I thought it was time to bring in the big guns, literally. Terence got into position and was ready to launch, when he saw Matilda and got too shy to do anything.

In the end, the only bird I could trust was me! I went to the island, knocked over the tower and came back with five eggs. Mission accomplished.

Update: Red only did this thanks to MY fancy new slingshot invention, thank you very much!

Stella xxx

1 Circle the correct answer.

a. How many eggs did Red want to bring back?

5   3   7

b. Who did Red send first?

Terence   Mighty Eagle   Chuck

c. Who did Terence see right before he was supposed to launch?

Matilda   Stella   Silver

d. Who was Mighty Eagle talking to?

Hal   Bubbles   The Blues

e. Who did Red need help from to save the eggs?

Stella   Silver   Matilda

2 Answer the following in a sentence or two.

a. Explain how Red felt when all the other birds had failed.

_____

_____

b. Why are the eggs so important to the birds?

_____

_____

CONJUCTIONS

The pigs love to use tools to put things together.

Just like the hammer and nails on the pig's construction site, conjunctions are special words used to glue together two parts of a sentence, phrase or clause.

Common conjunctions include:

and	or	but	so	because	after
until	yet	if	when	since	while

Conjunctions can come at the start of the sentence or in the middle.

When something is broken in the house, I like to get out my toolbox.

Here, the conjunction comes at the start of the sentence. There is a comma in the middle which separates the two clauses.

I like to get out my toolbox when something is broken in the house.

Here, the sentence has been rewritten with the conjunction put in the middle.

1 Rewrite these sentences with the conjunction in the middle:

a. Before I go to bed, I always brush my teeth.

_____

b. After I tell a joke, everyone laughs.

_____

c. While I'm writing my poetry, everyone is always talking.

_____

2 From the table at the top of the page, choose a suitable conjunction to complete these sentences:

a. Courtney came up with a great idea _____ she put down her phone for five minutes.

b. Chef Pig decided to serve dinner _____ the pigs had finished their latest tower.

c. Leonard builds towers _____ he wants to protect his stolen eggs.

d. Garry hid _____ the island was under attack.

SPELLING PATTERN -SION

We all know who makes the biggest explosions on the island. It's your friend and mine ... Bomb!

-sion can be a tricky word ending. If a word ending is pronounced "shun" then the spelling pattern will be -sion. **Top tip:** listen carefully as you say the words.

1 Put the **-sion** ending on the word beginnings and match them to the pictures.

Colli-

Inva-

Explo-

Obses-   **-sion**

Confu-

Vi-

a. _____

b. _____

c. _____

d. _____

e. _____

f. _____

2 Complete the sentences with a **-sion** word.

a. Let's watch _____ tonight.

b. Be careful as Garry's experiment might cause an _____ .

c. Garry's _____ is blurry without his glasses.

d. Hal and Bubbles banged heads in their _____ .

explosion

vision

television

collision

ANGRY BIRDS

MAKING PREDICTIONS

Chef Pig loves to predict what disastrous plan Leonard and his team will come up with next.

A **prediction** is using what you already know about the people and situation to make a reasonable estimation of what might happen next.

1 Think about this situation: Leonard has told the Bad Piggies to think of different materials they can use to make super strong towers. They have decided to use some items they have found around Piggy Island. They predict they will be strong enough.

Can you write three alternative predictions of what could happen?

1. _____

2. _____

3. _____

2 Look at these pictures and predict what might happen next:

SPELLING TRICKY WORDS

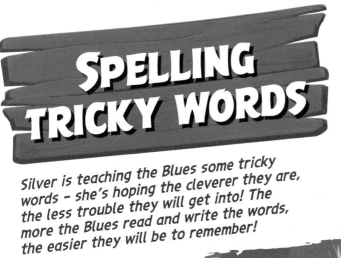

Silver is teaching the Blues some tricky words – she's hoping the cleverer they are, the less trouble they will get into! The more the Blues read and write the words, the easier they will be to remember!

1 Help the Blues use the letter clues in the crossword to insert the tricky words.

February   people

circle   recent   cousin

swimming   received

Crossword:
- 3 across: _ _ e _ r _ _ _ _ 4 r
- 5 across: _ _ e _ 6 _ _ _ _ e _ _ _
- 6 down: s
- 7 across: _ _ i _ _ _ _

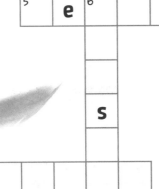

Use some of the words above to fill in the blanks in these sentences.

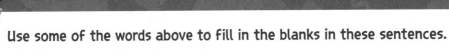

2

a. The month after January is _____ .

b. Butterfly and front crawl are both _____ strokes.

c. The teacher asked the children to sit in a _____ .

d. When are you visiting your _____ ?

e. Some _____ like to wear sunglasses.

PREPOSITIONS

ANGRY BIRDS

The Hatchlings can be quite shy, so they are hiding behind Matilda.

Behind shows the position of the Hatchlings in relation to Matilda. The word **behind** is a **preposition**. A preposition shows how a noun or pronoun is related to another word in a sentence. Prepositions often relate to the location that something is in, like the example above.

1

Circle the **preposition** in each of these sentences.

a. The birds soar above Bird Island.

b. The eggs are under the tower.

c. Red stood next to Chuck.

d. The birds take off between two trees.

e. Mighty Eagle lives inside Eagle Mountain.

2

Look at these words and identify the missing **prepositions** in the sentences.

beside   on   under   in   next

a. Zeta is floating _____ a bed of ice.

b. Matilda is walking _____ the grass.

c. The Hatchlings sleep _____ to each other.

d. Bird Island and Piggy Island are _____ each other.

e. Hal has a nap _____ a big tree.

PREFIX RE-

Terence has come up with a letter to tell Matilda how he really feels about her. He wants it to be perfect so he revisits his letter each day. He constantly reviews what he has written and sometimes can't recall what he actually wants to say!

Prefixes are groups of letters put in front of a root verb which will change the meaning of the word. The prefix re- means do again. Re+write = rewrite. Rewrite means to write again.

1 The **prefix re-** can be used in front of some verbs to make a new word but not all verbs make sense with a re- prefix. Sort these words into the correct column in the table. The first one has been done for you.

resleep   ~~reeat~~   return   redance   rerun   refish   replay   reheat

Makes a new word	Does not make a new word
	reeat

2 Use the words below to fill in the blanks in these sentences:

reappeared

replays

reheated

remade

retold

a. The pigs _____ their tower after it was destroyed.

b. Courtney _____ her favourite video on her phone.

c. The Blues _____ out of nowhere.

d. Mighty Eagle _____ the same story.

e. Chef Pig _____ dinner when the pigs were late.

PREPOSITIONS

Chuck likes to get up early for a pre-breakfast zoom around the island. The rest of the birds like to snooze in their nests instead.

> Prepositions are words that tell us **where (place)** or **when (time)** something is happening in relation to something else.

1

Complete the sentences below using the correct time preposition.

before	during	until
When he wakes up	after	

a. Chuck goes to bed _____ the rest of the birds - he wants to be well rested.

b. Red and Matilda cook breakfast _____ Chuck's flight.

c. Chuck keeps zooming _____ he runs out of energy.

d. _____ , Bomb likes to watch Chuck flying above him.

e. Chuck goes for a refreshing bird bath _____ his flight.

2

Sort these prepositions into time and place. Colour in **prepositions of place (where)** in red and **prepositions of time (when)** in blue.

on Monday	later	after
beyond	underneath	during
beside	before	next to

Read the sentences and circle the type of preposition which is used.

a. It has been one day since the pigs last tried to kidnap the eggs.　　**Time / Place**

b. Chef Pig told no one to come near the kitchen while he was preparing his feast.　　**Time / Place**

c. Bubbles couldn't help eating all the sweets in Matilda's pantry!　　**Time / Place**

d. Hal fell over three times before lunch.　　**Time / Place**

SUFFIX -LY

While the Hatchlings are sleeping quietly, the birds know they must flutter gently, not speak loudly and behave calmly, so they don't wake them.

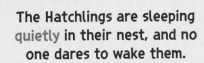

A **suffix** is a group of letters put on the end of a word. Adding the suffix **-ly** to a word changes it from an adjective to an adverb. An **adverb** describes how an action is done.

The Hatchlings are sleeping **quietly** in their nest, and no one dares to wake them.

Quiet + ly = Quietly

1 Change these adjectives into adverbs by adding the **-ly** suffix. The first one has been done for you.

adjective	adverb
brave	bravely
quiet	
calm	
bold	
exact	
glad	

2 Have a look what happens when the word ends in **y** or **e**, and you add the **-ly** suffix.

happy
happy + ly = happily

gentle
gentle + ly = gently

Explain what happens.

<u>Hint:</u> Notice what happened to the letter y on the end of happy.

_____

_____

_____

3 Use the following adverbs in a sentence:

calmly _____

happily _____

gently _____

PLOT LINES

Stella has decided that Bird Island is looking a bit shabby and wants to give it a makeover, but Red likes things just the way they are!

Plot lines for stories have elements which see the story build up to a problem, the problem is then solved and is followed by an ending. Have a look at the Angry Birds situation below and plot out the story.

1 How will Stella plan to change the Island and what will Red do to stop her? Will Stella go too far, or will Red like what she does?

Story start	Build up	Challenge and problem	The problem solved	Ending/ resolution
Stella decides to make changes on the island.	Red finds out and is not happy.			

2 Use your plan to write your story. Make sure you use plenty of description so that the reader gets a clear picture of what is happening and you create a sense of atmosphere. Continue on a piece of paper if you run out of space.

WRITING PRACTICE

The pigs want to show Leonard just how much they have learned. They are going to write a report on their latest structure in their best handwriting.

Handwriting should be neat and consistent in size. All ascending letters should be the same height and all descending letters should be the same length.

1 Can you help the pigs write their report using your best handwriting?

This is a report on our latest tower. It was at least 58 eggs' tall and 14 eggs wide.

We made the tower out of wood and steel rods. We ran out of nails half way through, so we used chewing gum instead.

The tower was a bit wobbly, but we think the rocking motion was quite soothing.

_____
_____
_____
_____
_____
_____
_____
_____
_____
_____

2 Leonard is going to mark the report using three words. What three words do you think he chose? Write them neatly below.

_____

PAST PERFECT TENSE

Chuck didn't believe that Stella could read a book faster than he could. After all, he is the fastest bird on the island. Chuck was only a few pages into his book when Stella cried: "I have finished!"

When shouting this, Stella used the past perfect tense. The past perfect tense uses **has** or **have** to show that something has happened but is still relevant now. For example – I **have** painted the room.

1 Complete these past perfect sentences by adding in a past tense verb. Choose the correct verb from the list. The first one has been done for you.

~~walk~~

cook

wash

talk

crash

a. "My wings were tired, so I have **walked** to Eagle Mountain," said Red.

b. Matilda has _____ to Terence for hours, he did not say much back.

c. Red was happy when the pigs tower _____ to the ground.

d. Hal has _____ the eggs to make them look shiny.

e. Bomb has _____ dinner for the rest of the birds.

2 Hal and Bubbles have been given some jobs to do around Bird Island by Red. Write a diary entry for Hal detailing the tasks they did that day using the past perfect tense. The diary has been started for you.

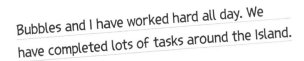

Bubbles and I have worked hard all day. We have completed lots of tasks around the Island.

- Sweeping feathers from the town square.

- Take Mighty Eagle's post up to Eagle Mountain.

- Help the Hatchlings go for their afternoon nap.

- Paint Red's fence.

READING COMPREHENSION

When it comes to Zeta and Mighty Eagle's past, let's just say 'it's complicated!'

Read Zeta's secret diary entry, then tick the correct answer box for the questions below. To answer the questions you will need to use **inference**. This means you will need to use **clues** and **evidence** in the text to form your thinking for your answers.

What a day! To think I have been living in that seal-infested frozen wasteland for so long, and now I have married the love of my life. Took him long enough. Years ago, Mighty Eagle and I were inseparable. We literally went everywhere together! I wanted to get married, but Mighty had other ideas. So, for years I waited, then I decided to use all that anger to get my own back and create a little paradise of my own. All I had to do was get rid of all the birds and all the pigs. Simple, right? Shame Red and the other birds weren't too happy with my plans... Who knew that would lead me to finally getting married! Red even performed the ceremony!

1 Why was Zeta angry at Mighty Eagle?

a. Because he insulted her feathers.

b. Because he stole her last fish.

c. Because he did not want to get married.

2 Why were the birds upset with Zeta?

a. Because she stole some eggs.

b. Because she wanted to take over the island.

c. Because she tells terrible jokes.

3 How did Red feel at the end of the diary entry?

a. Angry.

b. Happy for Zeta and Mighty Eagle.

c. Bored.

4 Explain why Zeta was cross with Mighty Eagle. Use evidence from the story to help you.

_____

HANDWRITING

Courtney has spent so long texting on her phone that she has forgotten how to do joined up handwriting. Can you help her?

When **handwriting**, some letters are joined using a diagonal stroke such as **ck** and some are joined with a horizontal stroke such as **oo**.

Some letters are best left **un-joined**. These include **capital letters** which **start sentences** and **names**.

1 Copy Courtney's letter to her friend in your best joined up handwriting.

_____

_____

_____

_____

_____

_____

Courtney's letter:

Leonard has been working me
super hard this week. He wants me to
take photos of him looking all King-like.
Eww. Know any filters for pigs with
really bad facial hair?

2 What else do you think Courtney will write in her letter?

_____

_____

_____

_____

PREFIXES MIS- AND DIS-

ANGRY BIRDS

Silver is showing the Hatchlings some word-magic. She is explaining how she can change the meaning of words!

Adding **prefixes** to the beginning of words changes their meaning. Adding the prefix **dis-** or **mis-** to a word will create a negative meaning, often the opposite of what it meant before.

In Silver's trick, she first makes a bunch of flowers **appear**. But then, using her prefix trick, adding the prefix **dis-** made the flowers **disappear**.

dis + appear = disappear

1 Which of the prefixes needs to be added to give the word the opposite meaning? Draw a line from the prefix to the correct root word. The first one has been done for you.

mis-

dis-

appear

agree

behave

spell

like

treat

loyal

believe

match

place

2 Silver has used her 'word magic' to make up the following words. Can you write each word into a sentence? The first one has been done for you.

 mismatch — Red found two trainers but they were a **mismatch**.

disagree _____

misbehave _____

dislike _____

misplace _____

PRONOUNS AND NOUNS

Matilda has just brought a new Hatchling to meet the birds...

"He's so cute!" screamed Hal.

"I think he looks like he's gonna be a wrecking ball when he grows up!" said Red, happily.

"Actually, he's not cute or a wrecking ball," said Matilda. "He is actually a she!"

"It doesn't matter," said Stella. "All Angry Birds and Angry Chicks are welcome on Bird Island!"

Nouns are words for people, places and things. **Pronouns** replace nouns to add variety and avoid repetition within a sentence. For example, instead of always using the noun **Red**, you could use the pronoun **he** in some sentences.

1 Sort the nouns and the pronouns below. Note: some pronouns are plural like 'they.'

Red	he	they	we
bird	Stella	Hal	ours
Matilda	myself		Hatchling

Nouns	Pronouns

2 Rewrite the sentence and change the **_underlined_** noun to a pronoun. The first one has been done for you.

a. Red was going to teach Terence a new move, so **_Red_** went to Terence's nest.	Red was going to teach Terence a new move, so **_he_** went to Terence's nest.
b. Stella is so cheerful, **_Stella_** always manages to put the birds in a good mood.	
c. King Pig wants to make the best tower yet, so **_King Pig_** asks to speak to Garry right away.	

29

CREATIVE WRITING

The Blues have decided to put on a play for the rest of the birds. First they want to write a script!

Scripts use a **narrator**, put the **speakers on the left**, contain **no speech marks** and stage directions are written in **brackets**.

1 The Blues have made a start on their play. Have a look at their script so far. Draw a line from the script element to where it is in the script.

Use of narrator

Speakers on the left

Stage directions in brackets

Narrator: It was a dark and stormy day on Bird Island. Three brave birds stepped out into the wind and rain.

Jake: We are the only ones strong enough to save the eggs!

Jay: We will brave the storm and land on Piggy Island. (Jay points to the sky)

Jim: And everyone will think we are so wonderful, we'll become the leaders of the birds! (Jim puts his wings on his hips)

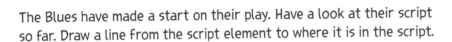

2 Think about what the Blues will write next. Will they be brave enough to make it through the storm? Will they need anyone else's help?

Character's name or narrator	What the character/narrator says and what the character does (written in brackets)

EXPANDED NOUN PHRASES

Something yummy is cooking in Chef Pig's kitchen! He's baked a cake, in fact, he's baked a light, fluffy cream cake with strawberry jam!

The second description of the cake sounds more delicious, doesn't it? That's because it is giving a bit more detail with an **expanded noun phrase**.

Expanded noun phases are phrases which **include an adjective or two to describe the noun.** For example, Chef Pig's cake versus Chef Pig's **light, fluffy** cream cake gives us more detail about what the cake is like.

Expanded noun phrases can also **tell us where the noun is.** For example, The cake is **ready in Chef Pig's kitchen.**

Expanded noun phrases help the reader to develop a clear picture in their head of what is written.

1 Underline the **adjectives** in these phrases. The first one has been done for you.

a. Courtney has a shiny, new phone.

b. Chef Pig's bright, white hat is missing.

c. Garry's experiment is explosively dangerous.

d. Leonard is in a dark, angry mood.

e. The pigs want fancy, new helmets.

f. The Bad Piggies lie down in a heap, utterly exhausted.

2 Underline the additional information about **where the noun is** in these sentences. The first one has been done for you.

a. The Piggies' dinner has been served in the dining room.

b. The stolen eggs have been hidden behind some rocks.

c. The plans for the new tower have been laid out on a table.

d. Leonard's crown has been locked in a safe.

e. The sun is setting over Piggy Island.

f. Garry's experiment has burned down the lab.

PARTS OF A SENTENCE

The pigs might all look like big, green egg-napping machines, but they each have their own job within the team.

Just like the pigs, words have differences too. **Nouns** are people, places and things. **Verbs** are action words. **Prepositions** are words that tell someone where or when something is in relation to something else. **Adjectives** are used to describe a noun and **adverbs** are used to describe a verb (how an action is done). When these different word types are put together, they make a successful sentence!

1 Look at the words below. Chef Pig is looking for the **nouns** - circle them in red. Courtney is looking for **verbs** - circle the verbs in blue.

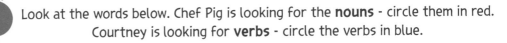

egg	Flying	run	chirping	plotting
tower	cooking	win	hiding
cheering	nest	feather	beak	snout

2 Help Stella and Silver to sort these **adjectives** and **adverbs** into their correct boxes. Draw a line from each word to its correct box.

quietly

quickly

clever

pink

slowly

long

adverb

adjective

3 Circle the correct **preposition** in the sentences below. The first one has been done for you.

a. Red is in / on the bath.

b. Chuck zooms over / under Bird Island.

c. Matilda meditates sitting on / over her favourite cushion.

d. Silver writes her notes under / in her best notebook.

e. The Hatchlings feel all cozy inside / outside the nest.

f. Mighty Eagle stares out from the top / bottom of Eagle Mountain.

SPELLING PATTERN -TION

When Red is ready to take ACTION, he makes his SELECTION from the birds. He wants to cause a COMMOTION and create as much DESTRUCTION as he can. Luckily, with such an amazing group of Birds, Red has lots of OPTIONS!

The spelling pattern **-tion** is easy. It is used to form a noun which means the action or result of a **verb**.

reflect   reflect + tion = reflection

Reflect is a verb (an action word) but adding the suffix **-tion** makes it a noun. Root words which end in **t** or **te** will usually be expanded with the **-tion** spelling pattern. The **t** or **te** is taken away, and the suffix **-tion** is added.

---

1 Expand these words with the **-tion** spelling pattern. The first one has been done for you.

Root word	Expanded word with -tion spelling pattern
act	action
animate	
donate	
disrupt	
instruct	
affect	
select	
rotate	

2 Add the correct **-tion** word for each sentence.

invitations   **eruption**   **affection**

operation   **imagination**

a. Terence has lots of _____ for Matilda.

b. Zeta wants to cause an _____ .

c. Red is coming up with ideas for the birds' next _____ .

d. Hal has a big _____ .

e. Stella is sending out _____ to the Hatchlings birthday party.

EDITING AND CORRECTING

Courtney is writing a post for the pig's social media pages. She wants it to be just right, so she's checking it before she presses 'post'.

Once a piece of work has been completed, it is important to check punctuation, sentence structure and use of description. There is usually always something which can be changed to make it even better!

Take a look at Courtney's post.

A day on Piggy Island

Today was a totally awesome day on Piggy Island. Some of the Bad Piggies stole.

eggs from Bird Island and we hid them. leonard was totally happy. I reckon we

will keep hold of them this time. The pigs are already building a tower to keep

them safe, although Leonard is getting cross at the Bad piggies.

1 Help Courtney to edit her report. Use the list below to help you check the text and add in any edits that are needed.

Item	Checked or Corrected
Capital letters: Sentences and proper nouns such as names start with a capital letter.	
Punctuation: Every sentence ends with a full stop and there are commas in a list. Questions have question marks.	
Sentence structure: There are longer complex sentences and shorter ones too. Can you join any sentences together to create a range of sentence lengths?	
Description: There are plenty of adjectives to interest the reader.	

PARAGRAPHS AND HEADINGS

Silver has written a report on how the birds behave each day. Can you help her to make her report more organised by using paragraphs and sub-headings?

Paragraphs are used to describe or explain an idea. New paragraphs are marked by starting a new line and are required when there is a change in theme. They make writing easier to read. In non-fiction writing, the paragraphs usually have **sub-headings**, which introduce what the next section of writing is about.

1 Help Silver by writing suitable sub-headings for her paragraphs. **Top tip:** Often a sub-heading is in the form of a question which will be answered in the paragraph that follows.

A week with the birds

Chuck gets up at 5am each day to fly laps of the island. By 10am, he is already exhausted!

Bomb is so afraid of setting himself off that he has asked Matilda to teach him meditation. He's not quite got the hang of it yet.

Mighty Eagle has not been seen for a few days. Chuck said he saw a large mirror being delivered to Eagle Island...

Stella wants me to stop working and hang out with her. So I'm going to!

2 The paragraphs have one main idea each. Read the statements below and decide if they are true or false.

a. Paragraph 1 is about Red.

True / False

b. Paragraph 2 is about Bomb and Matilda.

True / False

c. Paragraph 3 is about Zeta's husband.

True / False

d. Paragraph 4 is about Hal.

True / False

READING COMPREHENSION

You'll need to look for clues like a detective to complete the activities on this page.

Terence is a bird of few words. In fact, he's a bird of NO words! For that reason, the rest of the Angry Birds have to work out what sort of mood Terence is in by using **inference**.

Carefully read the paragraphs opposite. They contain clues which indicate what is about to happen but it doesn't tell us EXACTLY what is going to happen. When you are reading, think about how the characters are feeling and acting. Use the clues and what you know to answer the questions. This is called **inference**.

Stella woke up early. She had been so excited for today that she had struggled to get to sleep the night before. She did not mind. Her birthday had finally arrived.

Stella jumped out of her bed and went to check the post box. It was empty, and Stella felt disappointed. She fluffed her feathers and decided to go and see some of her friends.

Matilda said "Good morning Stella! Got to rush, I'm watching the Hatchlings today!"

Stella was confused. She was sure Matilda would have remembered!

Then, she saw Hal and Bubbles. They were whispering about something and stopped as soon as they saw Stella. "Oh, hi!" said Bubbles.

"Sorry, can't chat!" said Hal.

Stella was feeling miserable until Chuck whizzed past her and dropped a note into her lap. "Meet us on the beach, from the Angry Birds."

1 Use **inference** to answer these questions.

a. How was Stella feeling when she woke up? Why do you think she was feeling like this?

_____

_____

b. Why was Stella disappointed when her friends did not stop to chat?

_____

_____

c. What do you think will happen on the beach?

_____

_____

DIRECT SPEECH

SCAN CODE

purple mash

Red has decided to write a book all about the Angry Birds and their adventures. He's making notes in his notebook about a typical day on Bird Island.

As we learnt before, inverted commas or speech marks surround direct speech. They **go directly around the actual words being said by the character.** Punctuation, such as a question mark, is placed inside the inverted commas. Imagine a speech bubble - the inverted commas act like a speech bubble.

1 Identify if Red's sentences are punctuated correctly.

a. "Who's hungry?" asked Matilda.   **correct / incorrect**

b. I have lost my favourite pencil "moaned Stella."   **correct / incorrect**

c. "I'm gonna make a HUGE explosion today!" said Bomb.   **correct / incorrect**

d. "Does anyone have any beak plasters? asked" Hal.   **correct / incorrect**

e. "I'm gonna beat the all time bird-speed record, said Chuck."   **correct / incorrect**

2 Rewrite the incorrectly punctuated sentences above next to the character who said them. Remember to add in the inverted commas and any other missed punctuation.

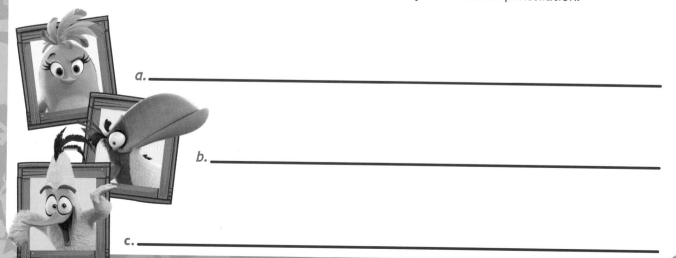

a. _____

b. _____

c. _____

PLURALS AND POSSESSIVES

Leonard likes nothing better than bossing the Bad Piggies around.

As we know, a noun is a person, place or thing. Adding an **s** to a noun will make it **plural**. This means there are more than one.

Pig   Pigs

Adding an **apostrophe** and an **s** to a noun means something belongs to the noun. This is called **possessive**.

The **Pig's skin** is green.

---

1 Look at the sentences. Circle to indicate if the **s** is used to make the noun a **plural** or a **possessive**.

a. **Courtney's** phone is low on battery.   **plural / possessive**

b. King Pig Leonard is obsessed with **eggs**.   **plural / possessive**

c. Chef Pig has lots of **pans**.   **plural / possessive**

d. **Garry's** coffee is hot and strong.   **plural / possessive**

e. **Chef's** hat is dirty.   **plural / possessive**

---

2 Can you help the Bad Piggies write a sentence for each of these nouns? The first one has been done for you.

a.

Tree	tree's (possessive)	The tree's leaves are turning brown.
	trees (plural)	There are plenty of trees on Piggy Island.

b.

Pencil	pencil's (possessive)	
	pencils (plural)	

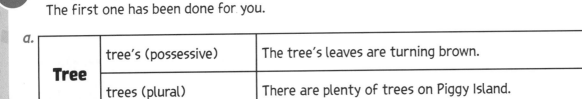

PLURAL APOSTROPHES

ANGRY BIRDS

Silver is creating a formula to help the birds zoom through the air even faster than they already do! She's written a list of strange items for the Blues to collect, but they are a bit confused by some of the items due to Silver's use of possessive apostrophes.

Possessive apostrophes can be a bit tricky if the noun is plural. **Plural** means when there is more than one.

If the owner noun is plural and **ends in s**, just add an apostrophe. For example, the wings which belong to the swarm of bees would be the **bees' wings**.

However, if the owner noun is plural and **does not end in s**, you add the apostrophe and the s. For example, toenails which belong to children (plural of child) would be the **children's toenails**.

1 Complete Silver's ingredients list using the correct possessive apostrophe. The first one has been done for you.

a.	Tears belonging to a group of seals	Seals' tears
b.	Eyelashes belonging to the pigs	
c.	Feathers belonging to a group of birds	
d.	Scales from a group of fish	

2 Rewrite the phrases below using a possessive apostrophe. The first one has been done for you.

a.	hair belonging to people	people's hair
b.	fleece belonging to sheep	
c.	feathers belonging to geese	
d.	earwax belonging to children	

FRONTED ADVERBIALS

Courtney is sending messages to the Piggy Kingdom on her phone. She wants to sound super smart so she wants to use fronted adverbials.

Adverbials are words or phrases which describe or give more information about the action in the sentence. They can describe how, when or where something happened. **Fronted adverbials** are adverbials found at the start of the sentence and are punctuated with a comma afterwards.

Leonard visited the stolen eggs **yesterday.**

Yesterday is the adverbial. It explains **when** the visit took place. The same sentence could be written with the adverbial at the start of the sentence. For example: **Yesterday,** Leonard visited the stolen eggs.

1

Rewrite Courtney's messages with the adverbial at the front.
HINT: Remember to add a comma!

a. A celebration for the stolen eggs will happen tomorrow evening.

_____

b. All Bad Piggies can now take their breaks on the beach.

_____

c. Egg stealing will now take place on Wednesdays.

_____

d. Chef Pig's lunch has disappeared mysteriously.

_____

2

Courtney was texting so quickly that she forgot to add the commas after the fronted adverbial. Put the commas in the correct place in the sentences below.

a. Early in the morning all was quiet in the palace.

b. Surprisingly the birds did not attack yesterday.

c. In two hours King Leonard will make an announcement.

POINT OF VIEW

Mighty Eagle is sharing his point of view because, well, he's Mighty Eagle and he thinks everyone will be interested!

The point of view in writing tells us about the perspective from which the story is being told. There are usually three viewpoints: first person, second person and third person.

Stories written in first person are told from the perspective of the character and use words such as I, me and we. Text written in second person involves the author addressing the reader. This is done using words like you, your and yours. In third person, the author acts as the narrator using the characters' names, he, she and they.

1

Rewrite these sentences about the Birds into first person.

a.

Third person:
Chuck is the fastest.

First person:

b.

Third person:
Bomb is feeling anxious.

First person:

c.

Third person:
Red is the leader.

First person:

2

Take a look at one of Mighty Eagle's stories and re-write it in first person.
Top tip: Pretend you are Mighty Eagle when you're writing.

Mighty Eagle was asked by Red to go and rescue some eggs from Piggy Island. Of course, he said yes, as he is a very kind and special bird. He spread his wings and flung himself into the attack.

_____
_____
_____
_____
_____

READING COMPREHENSION

Silver and Chuck are writing a letter home to their parents. They both have quite a lot to say! Read the letter, then have a go at answering the questions below.

Dear Mum and Dad AND ANYONE ELSE NOSY ENOUGH TO READ THIS LETTER.

We have had a lovely week on Bird Island. HAS IT BEEN A WEEK? IT FEELS LIKE TWO MINUTES!

Chuck was part of a rescue mission to Piggy Island. THAT'S ME - SUPERSTAR SON! Unfortunately he arrived three hours early. HEY, IT'S GOOD TO BE PREPARED!

I'm working on a machine that's 10 x stronger than the catapult. SHOW OFF. Red thinks we'll be able to put it to the test soon. OH, IGNORE THAT LAST COMMENT. CAN I HAVE A GO ON YOUR NEW SUPER CHARGED CATAPULT PLEASE? No. Maybe. Oh, go on then.

Miss you lots! WHEN ARE YOU COMING TO VISIT?

Silver & CHUCK.

---

1 Circle the correct answer.

a. Who writes first?

Silver   Chuck

b. How did Silver describe their week?

Busy   Boring   Lovely

c. How does Chuck describe himself?

Silly Son

Superstar Son

Superduper Son

---

2 Use your opinion to answer these questions:

a. Do Silver and Chuck get along? Explain why you think this way.

_____

b. How are Chuck and Silver different? Explain how.

_____

c. Do you think Chuck and Silver like their parents? Explain why.

_____

---

3 Use inference (clues from the text and what you already know) to answer the following questions:

a. Why does Chuck change his mind at the end of the letter?

_____

_____

b. How does Silver know the machine is almost ready?

_____

_____

ANGRY BIRDS

SPELLING
TRICKY WORDS

It's not just the Hatchlings who need to learn how to spell tricky words - even the grown-up Birds get these wrong from time to time!

1 Begin by circling the correct spelling of the words below:

a.	grammar	or	grammer
b.	axcident	or	accident
c.	sentanse	or	sentence
d.	reign	or	reegn
e.	February	or	Februry
f.	ayth	or	eighth
g.	naughty	or	nawghty
h.	library	or	librery
i.	knowledge	or	nowlidge

2 Take a look at these sentences below. Underline the spelling mistake in each one, then write in the correct spelling. The first one has been done for you.

a. It's been a whole week since Hal had an <u>axcident</u>.

_____accident_____

b. The Blues have been particularly nawghty this week.

_____

c. Silver has been spending a lot of time in the librery.

_____

d. Leonard has had a long reegn as king of Piggy Island.

_____

3 The Hatchlings are getting tired. They've started to miss out some letters in their spelling test! Can you help them to fill in the blanks to get full marks?

a. g r a _ _ _ r   e. F e b _ _ a r y

b. e _ _ h t h   f. n _ _ g h t _

c. s _ n t e n _ _   g. k n _ _ l e _ _ _

d. r _ _ g n   h. l i b _ a _ _

CINQUAIN POETRY

Leonard has decided the pigs need to learn Cinquain poetry to make them more cultured!

Leonard
Ruler of all
Stomping, bossing, shouting
Being the best Piggy ever
King Pig

Cinquain poems only have five lines, but each line has a particular number of syllables.

Line 1	Two syllables (which is also the title)
Line 2	Four syllables
Line 3	Six syllables (often ending in *ing*)
Line 4	Eight syllables
Line 5	Two syllables

Courtney
Top assistant
Helping, sorting, texting
No one knows what her job is too
Gen Z

1 Can you help Leonard write a Cinquain poem about another of the pigs?

Line 1	Two syllables (which is also the title)	
Line 2	Four syllables	
Line 3	Six syllables (often ending in ing)	
Line 4	Eight syllables	
Line 5	Two syllables	

2 Write out your poem in neat handwriting.

FRONTED ADVERBIALS

The birds can be super-competitive when it comes to how many towers they have knocked down. They all want to be first!

Just like Chuck, fronted adverbials always come first! They belong at the start of the sentence and give information about the verb in the sentence.

Fronted adverbial + comma + main clause

As we know, fronted adverbials can describe *time* (when something happened), *manner* (how something happened) or *place* (where something happened).

1

Add these fronted adverbials into the chart to show what they are describing. It could be time, manner or place.

next year	without warning	as fast as he could	back at Eagle Island
after a while	on the beach	awkwardly	far away	on saturday

time - when	manner - how	place - where
Every Monday	Quickly	Leonard's palace
During the afternoon	Carefully	Bird Island
When I wake up	Dazed and confused	Piggy Island

When using a fronted adverbial at the beginning of a sentence, it must always be followed by a comma.

2

Look at these sentences with fronted adverbials. Circle whether the comma is in the correct place or not.

a. On Monday, afternoon Red decided to take on the Pigs' tower on his own. correct / incorrect

b. Carefully, Garry experimented until he found the perfect gadget. correct / incorrect

c. Quick as a flash, Chuck jumped into action. correct / incorrect

d. Unexpectedly there was, an attempted egg robbery! correct / incorrect

ANSWERS

Page 2: Parts of a sentence

1. **Nouns:** egg, Chuck, pig, beak, feathers, catapult, snout, sunglasses, eyebrows, tower, bricks, Red, trotters, bomb, moustache, Matilda
   Verbs: flying, breaking, smashing, building, squawking, bricks, snorting, catching, playing

2. black, huge, stretchy, precious, calmest

3. **The chosen word should describe the verb. Examples could include:**
   a. The pigs build their towers quickly.
   b. The blues land roughly.
   c. Red leads the birds bravely.
   d. Silver quietly works on her homework.

Page 3: Handwriting practice

1 & 2. Accept any handwriting where the ascenders and descenders do not touch and are spaced appropriately.

Page 4: Homophones and Near Homophones

1. pear – pair
   meat – meet
   ball – bawl
   break – brake
   great – grate
   herd – heard
   knight – night
   blue – blew

2. a. meet   c. blew   e. missed
   b. heard   d. great

3. quiet – quite
   were – where
   further – father
   except – accept
   bury – berry

Page 5: Reading comprehension

1. a. false   c. false   e. true
   b. true   d. true   f. true

2. a. The bakery, the Bird Boutique and the Bubble Tea stand.
   b. An answer which refers to Terence showing how much he cares for Matilda.
   c. An answer which explains that Terence gave his time to sit and listen to Matilda.

Page 6: Direct speech

1. a. "I need a new job, fast," said Chef Pig.
   b. "Is anyone paying attention to my lastest invention?" asked Garry.
   c. "Has anyone seen my phone charger?" asked Courtney.
   d. "Nearly time for lunch!" said Chef Pig.
   e. "I need more eggs!" shouted Leonard.

2. Accept any words which have the same or similar meaning to said.

Page 7: Indefinite articles

1. A list with 6 of the following:
   an aeroplane, a rollercoaster, an umbrella, a pig, a boulder, a windmill, a ball pit, a lounger, a box of TNT.

2. a. an x-ray   c. a uniform
   b. an honour   d. an hour

Page 8: Spelling pattern -cian

1. a. optician   d. magician
   b. physician   e. electrician
   c. musician   f. beautician

2. a. politician   c. technician
   b. mathematician   d. dietician

Page 9: Similes

1. Red - As red as a ripe cherry.
   Bomb - Louder than thunder.
   Matilda - Loves her eggs as much as mice love cheese.
   Hal - A beak as big as a boomerang.
   Mighty Eagle - As proud as a peacock.
   Chuck - As fast as lightning.

2. Any suitable similes which make sense in the sentence.

Page 10: Alphabetical order

1. Hal, Matilda, Stella
2. Blues, Bomb, Bubbles
3. Chloe, Chunk

Page 11: Word families

1. Family 1: tricycle, tripod, triangle
   Family 2: television, telescope, telephone
   Family 3: microscope, microphone, microwave

2. micro – small   tri – three
   tele – distant

Page 12: Prefixes

1. **super**market   **mid**night
   impossible   **im**polite
   indoors   **mis**place
   superstar   **in**complete
   superman   **un**usual
   nonsense   **un**equal

2. super - man - **superman**
   re - write - rewrite
   in - dependent - **independent**
   im - mature - **immature**
   im - patient - impatient
   super - **star** - superstar
   non - sense - **nonsense**
   un - equal - unequal

Page 13: Direct speech

1. a. Hal asked, "What did Matilda say to the cat about their handwriting?"
      "I don't know," sighed Red.
      "It's paw-fect!" snorted Hal.
   b. "What is sticky and brown?" Hal giggled.
      "I don't know, you tell me!" Red replied.
      "A stick! Hahaha!" laughed Hal.

2. "I've got a great idea! Let's sneak up to eagle mountain," whispered Riley.

   "Excellent idea! We can listen to all of Mighty Eagle's interesting stories." chuckled Will.

Page 14: Reading comprehension

1. a. five   c. Matilda   e. Stella
   b. Chuck   d. The Blues

2. a. Any suitable answer which explains that Red was determined to get the eggs back and wouldn't give up.
   b. Any suitable answer which explains that the eggs and the hatchlings are precious to the birds.

Page 15: Conjunctions

1. a. I always brush my teeth before I go to bed.
   b. Everyone laughs after I tell a joke.
   c. Everyone is always talking while I'm writing my poetry

2. a. when   c. because
   b. after   d. while

Page 16: Spelling pattern -sion

1. a. explosion
   b. confusion
   c. invasion
   d. obsession
   e. vision
   f. collision

2. a. television
   b. explosion
   c. vision
   d. collision

Page 17: Making predictions

1. Any alternative prediction that relate to Leonard and the Bad Piggies such as, 'I predict that Leonard and the pigs won't use different materials' or 'I predict the towers won't be very strong.'

2. Any predictions related to the images.

Page 18: Spelling tricky words

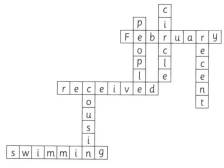

2. a. February
   b. swimming
   c. circle
   d. cousin
   e. people

Page 19: Prepositions

1. a. The birds soar **above** bird island.
   b. The eggs are **under** the tower.
   c. Red stood **next to** Chuck.
   d. The birds take off **between** two trees.
   e. Mighty Eagle lives **inside** Eagle Mountain.
2. a. Zeta is floating **on** a bed of ice.
   b. Matilda walking **through** the grass.
   c. The Hatchlings sleep **next** to each other.
   d. Bird Island and Piggy Island are **beside** each other.
   e. Hal has a nap **under** a big tree.

Page 20: Prefix re-

1. **Makes new words:**
   rerun, return, replay, reheat
   Does not makes new words:
   reeat, redance, resleep, refish
2. a. The pigs remade their tower after it was destroyed.
   b. Courtney replays here favourite video on her phone.
   c. The Blues reappeared out of nowhere.

d. Mighty Eagle retold the same story.
e. Chef Pig reheated dinner when the pigs were late.

Page 21: Prepositions

1. a. before
   b. during
   c. until
   d. When he wakes up
   e. after

2.

on Monday	later	after
beyond	underneath	during
beside	before	next to

3. a. time
   b. place
   c. place
   d. time

Page 22: Suffix -ly

1. bravely, quietly, calmly, boldly, exactly, gladly

2. The y in happy changes to an i before adding -ly and the e in gentle is removed before adding -ly.

3. Accept any sentences which make sense and include the adverbs.

Page 23: Plot lines

1. Table filled in with plausible ideas.

2. Story plotted with sufficient detail to keep the reader engaged.

Page 24: Writing practice

1. Accept neat joined up handwriting which is consistent in size and formation.

2. Accept a title. Capitals not joined but lower case letters joined.

Page 25: Past perfect tense

1. a. walked
   b. talked
   c. crashed
   d. washed
   e. cooked

2. Accept any sentences with past perfect tense.

Page 26: Reading comprehension

1. The correct answer is c
2. The correct answer is b
3. The correct answer is b
4. A written answer which explains why Zeta was feeling cross due to the fact she wanted to get married but Mighty Eagle didn't want to and she has been waiting for him.

Page 27: Handwriting

1 & 2. Accept handwriting where capitals stand alone and other letters are appropriately joined with either a diagonal or horizontal stroke.

Page 28: Prefixes mis- and dis-

1. **dis:** disappear, disagree, dislike, disloyal, disbelieve
   mis: misbehave, mistreat, mismatch, misspell, misplace

2. Accept any suitable sentences containing the given words.

Page 29: Pronouns and nouns

1. **nouns:** Red, bird, Matilda, Hal, Stella, Hatchling
   pronouns: he, they, ours, we, myself

2. a. Red was going to teach Terence a new move, so **he** went to Terence's nest.
   b. Stella is so cheerful, **she** always manages to put the birds in a good mood.
   c. King Pig wants to make the best tower yet, so **he** asks to speak to Garry right away.

Page 30: Creative writing

1. **Use of narrator:** pointing to the lines said by the narrator.
   Speakers on the left: pointing to names.
   Stage directions: pointing to the stage directions in brackets.

2. Accept any script with use of narrator, character's names on the left and what they say on the right, their actions in brackets.

Page 31: Expanded noun phrases

1. a. shiny, new
   b. bright, missing
   c. explosively, dangerous
   d. dark, angry
   e. fancy, new
   f. utterly, exhausted

2. a. in the dining room
   b. behind some rocks
   c. on a table
   d. locked in a safe
   e. over Piggy Island
   f. down the lab

Page 32: Parts of a sentence

1. **Nouns:** egg, tower, nest, feather, beak, snout
   Verbs: flying, run, chirping, plotting, cooking, win, hiding, cheering

2. **Adjectives:** pink, long, clever
   Adverbs: quietly, quickly, slowly

3. a. in
   b. over
   c. on
   d. in
   e. inside
   f. top

Page 33: Spelling pattern -tion

1. action, animation, donation, disruption, instruction, affection, selection, rotation

2. a. affection
   b. eruption
   c. operation
   d. imagination
   e. invitations

Page 34: Editing and correcting

1. **Example:** Today was a totally awesome day on Piggy Island. Some of the Bad Piggies stole eggs from Bird Island and we hid them. Leonard was totally happy. I reckon we will keep hold of them this time. The Pigs are already building a strong tower to keep them safe, although Leonard is getting cross at the Bad Piggies.

Page 35: Paragraphs and headings

1. Who wakes up first?
   Who is most explosive?
   Who is in love with himself?
   Who wants me to stop writing?
   (or similar)

2. a. false
   b. true
   c. true
   d. false

Page 36: Reading comprehension

1. a. She was excited because she was looking forward to her birthday. She could be tired because she didn't sleep well.

   b. She thought her friends were ignoring her and had forgotten her birthday.

   c. There will be a party on the beach and all of her friends will be there.

Page 37: Direct speech

1. a. correct
   b. incorrect
   c. correct
   d. incorrect
   e. incorrect

2. a. "I have lost my favourite pencil," moaned Stella.
   b. "Does anyone have any beak plasters?" asked Hal.
   c. "I'm gonna beat the all time bird-speed record," said Chuck.

Page 38: Plurals and possessives

1. a. possessive
   b. plural
   c. plural
   d. possessive
   e. possessive

2. Accept any correct sentences where pencil has been used both as a possessive and a plural.

Page 39: Plural apostrophes

1. a. seals' tears
   b. birds' feathers.
   c. pigs' eyelashes
   d. fish's scales.

2. a. people's hair
   b. sheep's fleece
   c. geese's feathers
   d. children's earwax

Page 40: Fronted adverbials

1. a. Tomorrow evening, a celebration for the stolen eggs will happen.
   b. On the beach, all Bad Piggies can now take their breaks.
   c. On Wednesdays, egg stealing will now take place.
   d. Mysteriously, Chef Pig's lunch has disappeared.

2. a. Early in the morning, all was quiet in the palace.
   b. Surprisingly, the Birds did not attack yesterday.
   c. In two hours, King Leonard will make an announcement

Page 41: Point of view

1. a. I am the fastest.
   b. I am feeling anxious.
   c. I am the leader.

2. I was asked by Red to go and rescue some eggs from Bird Island. Of course, I said yes, as I am a very kind and special bird. I spread my wings and flung myself into the attack.

Page 42: Reading comprehension

1. a. Silver
   b. lovely
   c. Superstar Son

2. Accept any answer which makes sense and is supported.

3. a. The super charged catapult sounds good and he wants to use it.
   b. Red thinks she will be able to put it to the test soon.

Page 43: Spelling tricky words

1. a. grammar
   b. accident
   c. sentence
   d. reign
   e. February
   f. eighth
   g. naughty
   h. library
   i. knowledge

2. a. accident
   b. naughty
   c. library
   d. reign

3. a. grammar
   b. eighth
   c. sentence
   d. reign
   e. February
   f. naughty
   g. knowledge
   h. library

Page 44: Cinquain poetry

1. Accept any suitable poem which matches the success criteria for a cinquain.

2. Accept the poem in best handwriting.

Page 45: Fronted adverbials

1. **Time:** Next year, After a while, On Saturday
   Manner: Without warning, Awkwardly, As fast as he could
   place: Back at Eagle Island, On the beach, Far away.

2. a. incorrect
   b. correct
   c. correct
   d. incorrect